50 Mac and More Recipes

By: Kelly Johnson

Table of Contents

- Classic Baked Mac and Cheese
- Buffalo Chicken Mac
- Mac and Cheese Pizza
- Lobster Mac and Cheese
- BBQ Pulled Pork Mac
- Jalapeño Popper Mac
- Bacon Cheeseburger Mac
- Truffle Mac and Cheese
- Broccoli Cheddar Mac
- Chili Mac Skillet
- Philly Cheesesteak Mac
- Cajun Shrimp Mac
- Garlic Parmesan Mac
- Taco Mac and Cheese
- Pesto Chicken Mac
- Sausage and Peppers Mac
- Mushroom Swiss Mac

- Meatball Marinara Mac
- Breakfast Mac with Eggs and Bacon
- Hot Honey Chicken Mac
- Spicy Sriracha Mac
- Chicken Alfredo Mac
- Cheeseburger Macaroni Bake
- Greek Mac with Feta and Olives
- Spinach and Artichoke Mac
- Ham and Swiss Macaroni Bake
- Southern-Style Mac with Collard Greens
- Chili Dog Mac
- Cheesesteak Mac Casserole
- Caprese Mac and Cheese
- Blue Cheese Bacon Mac
- Kimchi Mac
- Enchilada Mac
- Butternut Squash Mac
- Cajun Andouille Mac
- Garlic Herb Mac

- Chicken Parm Mac
- Sweet Corn Mac and Cheese
- Sloppy Joe Mac
- Ratatouille Mac
- Pepperoni Pizza Mac
- Tex-Mex Mac Skillet
- Mac and Cheese Stuffed Peppers
- Vegan Cashew Mac
- Korean BBQ Mac
- Gnocchi Mac and Cheese
- Reuben Mac Casserole
- Mac and Cheese Egg Rolls
- Fried Mac and Cheese Balls
- Mac and Cheese Waffles

Classic Baked Mac and Cheese

Ingredients:

- 1 lb elbow macaroni
- 4 cups milk
- 1/4 cup butter
- 1/4 cup flour
- 2 cups sharp cheddar, shredded
- 1 cup mozzarella, shredded
- 1 tsp mustard powder
- Salt, pepper, and garlic powder
- 1/2 cup breadcrumbs (optional)

Instructions:

1. Preheat oven to 350°F (175°C).
2. Cook pasta according to package directions and set aside.
3. In a saucepan, melt butter, then whisk in flour to make a roux.
4. Gradually add milk, whisking to prevent lumps, and cook until thickened.
5. Stir in cheeses, mustard powder, and seasonings.
6. Combine pasta and cheese sauce, then transfer to a greased baking dish.
7. Top with breadcrumbs (if using) and bake for 20–25 minutes until bubbly.

Buffalo Chicken Mac

Ingredients:

- 1 lb elbow macaroni
- 2 cups shredded cooked chicken
- 1/2 cup buffalo sauce
- 2 cups shredded cheddar
- 1/2 cup cream cheese
- 1 cup milk
- 1/2 tsp garlic powder
- Blue cheese crumbles (optional)

Instructions:

1. Preheat oven to 350°F (175°C).
2. Cook pasta and set aside.
3. In a saucepan, combine buffalo sauce, cream cheese, and milk. Stir until smooth.
4. Mix in shredded chicken, garlic powder, and 1 cup cheddar.
5. Toss pasta with the sauce, transfer to a baking dish, and top with remaining cheese.
6. Bake for 20 minutes or until bubbly. Garnish with blue cheese crumbles if desired.

Mac and Cheese Pizza

Ingredients:

- 1 pizza dough (store-bought or homemade)
- 2 cups cooked mac and cheese (your favorite recipe!)
- 1/2 cup mozzarella, shredded
- 1/4 cup parmesan, grated
- 1 tbsp olive oil

Instructions:

1. Preheat oven to 475°F (245°C).
2. Roll out pizza dough and brush with olive oil.
3. Spread a layer of mac and cheese over the dough.
4. Sprinkle with mozzarella and parmesan.
5. Bake for 10–12 minutes until golden and crispy.
6. Slice and enjoy the cheesy combination!

Lobster Mac and Cheese

Ingredients:

- 1 lb elbow macaroni
- 1/2 lb cooked lobster meat, chopped
- 4 cups milk
- 1/4 cup butter
- 1/4 cup flour
- 2 cups sharp cheddar, shredded
- 1 cup Gruyère, shredded
- Salt, pepper, and paprika
- Fresh parsley, chopped (for garnish)

Instructions:

1. Preheat oven to 350°F (175°C).
2. Cook pasta and set aside.
3. In a saucepan, melt butter, then whisk in flour to make a roux.
4. Gradually add milk, whisking to prevent lumps. Stir in cheeses until smooth.
5. Season with salt, pepper, and paprika.
6. Fold in lobster meat and pasta.
7. Pour into a greased baking dish, top with more cheese, and bake for 20–25 minutes.

8. Garnish with fresh parsley before serving.

BBQ Pulled Pork Mac

Ingredients:

- 1 lb elbow macaroni
- 2 cups pulled pork (cooked)
- 1 cup barbecue sauce
- 2 cups sharp cheddar, shredded
- 1/2 cup milk
- 1/4 cup sour cream
- Salt, pepper, and onion powder

Instructions:

1. Preheat oven to 350°F (175°C).
2. Cook pasta and set aside.
3. In a saucepan, mix barbecue sauce, milk, sour cream, and seasonings. Heat until combined.
4. Stir in pulled pork and cheddar, then mix with pasta.
5. Pour into a greased baking dish, top with more cheddar, and bake for 20 minutes until bubbly.

Jalapeño Popper Mac

Ingredients:

- 1 lb elbow macaroni
- 4 oz cream cheese
- 1/2 cup sour cream
- 1/2 cup shredded cheddar
- 2-3 jalapeños, diced
- 1/4 cup bacon bits
- 1/2 cup panko breadcrumbs
- Salt and pepper

Instructions:

1. Cook pasta and set aside.
2. In a saucepan, melt cream cheese with sour cream, cheddar, and jalapeños.
3. Stir in pasta and bacon.
4. Transfer to a baking dish, top with panko, and bake at 375°F (190°C) for 20 minutes or until bubbly.

Bacon Cheeseburger Mac

Ingredients:

- 1 lb elbow macaroni
- 1/2 lb ground beef
- 1/2 cup ketchup
- 1/2 cup mustard
- 1 cup cheddar cheese, shredded
- 1/4 cup pickles, diced
- 1/4 cup crispy bacon, crumbled
- Salt, pepper, and onion powder

Instructions:

1. Cook pasta and set aside.
2. Brown ground beef in a skillet with seasoning. Stir in ketchup and mustard.
3. Mix in cooked pasta, cheddar, pickles, and bacon.
4. Serve hot and enjoy this burger-inspired dish!

Truffle Mac and Cheese

Ingredients:

- 1 lb elbow macaroni
- 4 cups milk
- 1/4 cup butter
- 1/4 cup flour
- 2 cups Gruyère cheese, shredded
- 1 cup Parmesan, grated
- 2 tbsp truffle oil
- Salt, pepper, and garlic powder

Instructions:

1. Cook pasta and set aside.
2. In a saucepan, make a roux with butter and flour. Add milk and cook until thickened.
3. Stir in cheeses and truffle oil.
4. Toss pasta in the sauce, season with salt and pepper, and serve.

Broccoli Cheddar Mac

Ingredients:

- 1 lb elbow macaroni
- 2 cups broccoli florets, steamed
- 2 cups sharp cheddar, shredded
- 1 cup milk
- 1/4 cup butter
- 1/4 cup flour
- Salt, pepper, and garlic powder

Instructions:

1. Cook pasta and steam broccoli.
2. Make a roux with butter and flour, then add milk and cook until thickened.
3. Stir in cheddar, salt, pepper, and garlic powder.
4. Toss pasta and broccoli in cheese sauce and serve warm.

Chili Mac Skillet

Ingredients:

- 1 lb elbow macaroni
- 1 lb ground beef
- 1 can chili beans
- 1 can diced tomatoes
- 1 cup cheddar cheese, shredded
- 1 tsp chili powder
- Salt and pepper

Instructions:

1. Cook pasta and set aside.
2. Brown ground beef in a skillet, then stir in chili beans, tomatoes, and chili powder.
3. Mix in cooked pasta, then top with cheese.
4. Simmer until cheese is melted and bubbly.

Philly Cheesesteak Mac

Ingredients:

- 1 lb elbow macaroni
- 1 lb beef steak (thinly sliced)
- 1 green bell pepper, sliced
- 1 onion, sliced
- 2 cups provolone cheese, shredded
- 1 cup cream cheese
- 1 cup beef broth
- Salt, pepper, and garlic powder

Instructions:

1. Cook pasta and set aside.
2. Sauté bell pepper and onion in a skillet. Add steak and cook through.
3. Stir in cream cheese and beef broth, then mix in cooked pasta.
4. Top with provolone and let it melt. Serve warm.

Cajun Shrimp Mac

Ingredients:

- 1 lb elbow macaroni
- 1 lb shrimp, peeled and deveined
- 1 tbsp Cajun seasoning
- 1/2 cup cream cheese
- 1/2 cup milk
- 1 cup cheddar cheese, shredded
- 1/4 cup green onions, sliced

Instructions:

1. Cook pasta and set aside.
2. Toss shrimp in Cajun seasoning and cook in a skillet.
3. In a saucepan, melt cream cheese, milk, and cheddar.
4. Mix pasta, shrimp, and cheese sauce. Top with green onions and serve.

Garlic Parmesan Mac

Ingredients:

- 1 lb elbow macaroni
- 4 cloves garlic, minced
- 1/2 cup butter
- 1 cup heavy cream
- 1 1/2 cups Parmesan cheese, grated
- Salt, pepper, and parsley

Instructions:

1. Cook pasta and set aside.
2. Sauté garlic in butter until fragrant.
3. Stir in heavy cream, Parmesan, salt, and pepper.
4. Toss pasta in sauce and garnish with parsley.

Taco Mac and Cheese

Ingredients:

- 1 lb elbow macaroni
- 1 lb ground beef
- 1 packet taco seasoning
- 1 cup cheddar cheese, shredded
- 1/2 cup salsa
- 1/2 cup sour cream
- Chopped cilantro (optional)

Instructions:

1. Cook pasta and set aside.
2. Brown ground beef and stir in taco seasoning.
3. Mix in salsa and sour cream, then add pasta and cheddar.
4. Serve garnished with cilantro.

Pesto Chicken Mac

Ingredients:

- 1 lb elbow macaroni
- 2 cups cooked chicken, shredded
- 1/2 cup pesto sauce
- 1 cup mozzarella, shredded
- 1/4 cup Parmesan cheese, grated

Instructions:

1. Cook pasta and set aside.
2. Mix pesto with chicken and toss with pasta.
3. Stir in mozzarella and Parmesan, then serve warm.

Sausage and Peppers Mac

Ingredients:

- 1 lb elbow macaroni
- 2 sausages (Italian or your choice), sliced
- 1 red bell pepper, sliced
- 1 yellow onion, sliced
- 2 cups mozzarella, shredded
- 1/2 cup marinara sauce
- Salt, pepper, and Italian seasoning

Instructions:

1. Cook pasta and set aside.
2. Sauté sausage, peppers, and onions until cooked through.
3. Stir in marinara sauce and cooked pasta.
4. Top with mozzarella and bake for 10 minutes until cheese is melted.

Mushroom Swiss Mac

Ingredients:

- 1 lb elbow macaroni
- 2 cups Swiss cheese, shredded
- 2 cups mushrooms, sliced
- 2 tbsp butter
- 1/2 cup heavy cream
- 1/4 cup grated Parmesan
- Salt, pepper, and thyme

Instructions:

1. Cook pasta and set aside.
2. Sauté mushrooms in butter until golden and soft.
3. Add heavy cream, Swiss cheese, Parmesan, salt, pepper, and thyme to the pan, cooking until the cheese melts.
4. Toss pasta in the creamy mushroom sauce and serve hot.

Meatball Marinara Mac

Ingredients:

- 1 lb elbow macaroni
- 12 meatballs, cooked
- 1 jar marinara sauce
- 2 cups mozzarella cheese, shredded
- 1/4 cup Parmesan, grated
- Fresh basil (optional)

Instructions:

1. Cook pasta and set aside.
2. Heat marinara sauce and add cooked meatballs.
3. Mix in pasta, then top with mozzarella and Parmesan.
4. Bake at 375°F (190°C) for 15–20 minutes until cheese is melted. Garnish with basil.

Breakfast Mac with Eggs and Bacon

Ingredients:

- 1 lb elbow macaroni
- 6 slices bacon, cooked and crumbled
- 2 eggs, scrambled
- 1/2 cup cheddar cheese, shredded
- 1/4 cup cream
- Salt, pepper, and garlic powder

Instructions:

1. Cook pasta and set aside.
2. Scramble eggs and set aside.
3. In a skillet, combine pasta, bacon, eggs, cheddar, cream, and seasonings.
4. Cook over medium heat until cheese is melted and creamy. Serve warm.

Hot Honey Chicken Mac

Ingredients:

- 1 lb elbow macaroni
- 2 chicken breasts, cooked and shredded
- 1/4 cup hot honey (or regular honey with chili flakes)
- 1/2 cup cream cheese
- 1 cup sharp cheddar, shredded
- 1/2 tsp smoked paprika

Instructions:

1. Cook pasta and set aside.
2. Toss shredded chicken in hot honey.
3. In a saucepan, melt cream cheese and cheddar, then stir in paprika and cooked chicken.
4. Mix with pasta and serve.

Spicy Sriracha Mac

Ingredients:

- 1 lb elbow macaroni
- 1/2 cup sriracha sauce
- 2 cups mozzarella cheese, shredded
- 1/4 cup cream cheese
- 1 tbsp soy sauce
- 1/2 tsp garlic powder
- Chopped green onions (optional)

Instructions:

1. Cook pasta and set aside.
2. In a saucepan, melt cream cheese and sriracha sauce, adding soy sauce and garlic powder.
3. Mix in mozzarella until melted.
4. Toss pasta in the spicy sauce and top with green onions if desired.

Chicken Alfredo Mac

Ingredients:

- 1 lb elbow macaroni
- 2 chicken breasts, cooked and sliced
- 1 cup heavy cream
- 1 cup Parmesan cheese, grated
- 1/4 cup butter
- 1 garlic clove, minced
- Salt, pepper, and Italian seasoning

Instructions:

1. Cook pasta and set aside.
2. Sauté garlic in butter until fragrant, then add heavy cream and Parmesan.
3. Stir in chicken, salt, pepper, and Italian seasoning.
4. Toss with pasta and serve warm.

Cheeseburger Macaroni Bake

Ingredients:

- 1 lb elbow macaroni
- 1 lb ground beef
- 1 cup ketchup
- 1 tbsp mustard
- 2 cups cheddar cheese, shredded
- 1/2 cup pickles, chopped
- 1/4 cup onions, chopped

Instructions:

1. Cook pasta and set aside.
2. Brown ground beef, then stir in ketchup, mustard, and onions.
3. Combine pasta, beef mixture, cheese, and pickles.
4. Transfer to a baking dish, top with more cheese, and bake at 375°F (190°C) for 20 minutes.

Greek Mac with Feta and Olives

Ingredients:

- 1 lb elbow macaroni
- 1/2 cup feta cheese, crumbled
- 1/4 cup black olives, chopped
- 1/2 cup cherry tomatoes, halved
- 1/4 cup olive oil
- 1 tsp oregano
- Salt, pepper, and fresh parsley

Instructions:

1. Cook pasta and set aside.
2. Toss pasta with olive oil, feta, olives, tomatoes, oregano, salt, and pepper.
3. Garnish with fresh parsley and serve.

Spinach and Artichoke Mac

Ingredients:

- 1 lb elbow macaroni
- 2 cups spinach, sautéed
- 1 can artichoke hearts, drained and chopped
- 1 cup cream cheese
- 1/2 cup Parmesan, grated
- 1 cup mozzarella, shredded
- Salt, pepper, and garlic powder

Instructions:

1. Cook pasta and set aside.
2. Sauté spinach and set aside.
3. In a saucepan, melt cream cheese, Parmesan, and mozzarella.
4. Stir in spinach, artichokes, and seasonings.
5. Toss with pasta and serve.

Ham and Swiss Macaroni Bake

Ingredients:

- 1 lb elbow macaroni
- 2 cups ham, cubed
- 2 cups Swiss cheese, shredded
- 1/2 cup cream
- 1/4 cup breadcrumbs
- Salt and pepper

Instructions:

1. Cook pasta and set aside.
2. In a saucepan, combine cream and Swiss cheese until melted.
3. Mix in ham, pasta, salt, and pepper.
4. Transfer to a baking dish, top with breadcrumbs, and bake at 375°F (190°C) for 20 minutes.

Southern-Style Mac with Collard Greens

Ingredients:

- 1 lb elbow macaroni
- 2 cups collard greens, cooked and chopped
- 1/2 cup smoked sausage, sliced
- 1 cup cheddar cheese, shredded
- 1/4 cup cream
- 1/2 tsp paprika
- Salt and pepper

Instructions:

1. Cook pasta and set aside.
2. Sauté sausage, then stir in collard greens and cream.
3. Mix in cheese, paprika, salt, and pepper.
4. Toss with pasta and serve warm.

Chili Dog Mac

Ingredients:

- 1 lb elbow macaroni
- 4 hot dogs, sliced
- 1 can chili
- 1 cup cheddar cheese, shredded
- 1/4 cup onions, diced
- 1/4 cup mustard
- 1/4 cup ketchup

Instructions:

1. Cook pasta and set aside.
2. Heat chili in a saucepan and stir in sliced hot dogs, mustard, and ketchup.
3. Mix in cooked pasta, then top with cheddar and onions.
4. Bake at 375°F (190°C) for 15 minutes or until bubbly.

Cheesesteak Mac Casserole

Ingredients:

- 1 lb elbow macaroni
- 1 lb ribeye steak, thinly sliced
- 1 green bell pepper, sliced
- 1 onion, sliced
- 1 cup provolone cheese, shredded
- 1/2 cup cheddar cheese, shredded
- 1 cup beef broth
- 1/4 cup Worcestershire sauce

Instructions:

1. Cook pasta and set aside.
2. Sauté bell pepper, onion, and steak in a skillet.
3. Stir in beef broth and Worcestershire sauce.
4. Mix pasta, cheese, and beef mixture in a casserole dish.
5. Bake at 375°F (190°C) for 20 minutes or until cheese is melted.

Caprese Mac and Cheese

Ingredients:

- 1 lb elbow macaroni
- 2 cups mozzarella cheese, shredded
- 1 cup cherry tomatoes, halved
- 1/4 cup fresh basil, chopped
- 1 tbsp balsamic glaze
- 1/2 cup Parmesan, grated

Instructions:

1. Cook pasta and set aside.
2. Melt mozzarella and Parmesan with a little cream or milk.
3. Stir in pasta, cherry tomatoes, and basil.
4. Drizzle with balsamic glaze and serve.

Blue Cheese Bacon Mac

Ingredients:

- 1 lb elbow macaroni
- 1/2 cup blue cheese, crumbled
- 1 cup cheddar cheese, shredded
- 1/4 cup cream
- 4 slices bacon, cooked and crumbled
- Salt, pepper, and garlic powder

Instructions:

1. Cook pasta and set aside.
2. In a saucepan, melt cheddar with cream, then stir in blue cheese, bacon, and seasonings.
3. Toss pasta in the sauce and serve.

Kimchi Mac

Ingredients:

- 1 lb elbow macaroni
- 1/2 cup kimchi, chopped
- 1 cup cheddar cheese, shredded
- 1/4 cup cream cheese
- 1 tbsp sesame oil
- 1 tbsp soy sauce

Instructions:

1. Cook pasta and set aside.
2. Sauté kimchi in sesame oil, then stir in cream cheese and soy sauce.
3. Add cheddar cheese and stir until melted.
4. Mix in pasta and serve.

Enchilada Mac

Ingredients:

- 1 lb elbow macaroni
- 1 lb ground beef
- 1 can enchilada sauce
- 1 cup cheddar cheese, shredded
- 1/2 cup sour cream
- 1/4 cup green onions, chopped

Instructions:

1. Cook pasta and set aside.
2. Brown ground beef and stir in enchilada sauce.
3. Mix pasta with beef and enchilada sauce, then top with cheddar cheese and sour cream.
4. Garnish with green onions and serve.

Butternut Squash Mac

Ingredients:

- 1 lb elbow macaroni
- 2 cups butternut squash, roasted and mashed
- 1 cup sharp cheddar cheese, shredded
- 1/4 cup cream
- 1 tsp nutmeg
- Salt and pepper

Instructions:

1. Cook pasta and set aside.
2. In a saucepan, combine butternut squash, cream, and cheddar until melted.
3. Season with nutmeg, salt, and pepper.
4. Toss pasta in the creamy sauce and serve.

Cajun Andouille Mac

Ingredients:

- 1 lb elbow macaroni
- 1/2 lb Andouille sausage, sliced
- 1 cup sharp cheddar cheese, shredded
- 1/2 cup heavy cream
- 1 tsp Cajun seasoning
- 1/4 cup green onions, chopped

Instructions:

1. Cook pasta and set aside.
2. Sauté Andouille sausage with Cajun seasoning.
3. Add heavy cream and cheddar, stirring until cheese melts.
4. Mix in pasta and top with green onions.

Garlic Herb Mac

Ingredients:

- 1 lb elbow macaroni
- 2 tbsp butter
- 4 cloves garlic, minced
- 1 cup Parmesan cheese, grated
- 1/4 cup cream
- 1 tsp Italian seasoning
- Fresh parsley, chopped

Instructions:

1. Cook pasta and set aside.
2. Sauté garlic in butter until fragrant.
3. Stir in cream, Parmesan, and Italian seasoning.
4. Toss pasta in sauce and garnish with fresh parsley.

Chicken Parm Mac

Ingredients:

- 1 lb elbow macaroni
- 2 chicken breasts, breaded and fried
- 1 jar marinara sauce
- 1 cup mozzarella cheese, shredded
- 1/4 cup Parmesan cheese, grated
- Fresh basil (optional)

Instructions:

1. Cook pasta and set aside.
2. Slice breaded chicken and set aside.
3. Heat marinara sauce and mix in pasta.
4. Top with sliced chicken, mozzarella, and Parmesan.
5. Bake at 375°F (190°C) for 15 minutes or until cheese is melted.

Sweet Corn Mac and Cheese

Ingredients:

- 1 lb elbow macaroni
- 1 cup sweet corn kernels (fresh or frozen)
- 2 cups cheddar cheese, shredded
- 1/2 cup cream cheese
- 1/4 cup butter
- Salt and pepper

Instructions:

1. Cook pasta and set aside.
2. Sauté corn in butter until lightly browned.
3. In a saucepan, melt cream cheese and cheddar.
4. Mix in corn and pasta, then season with salt and pepper.

Sloppy Joe Mac

Ingredients:

- 1 lb elbow macaroni
- 1 lb ground beef
- 1 can sloppy joe sauce
- 1 cup cheddar cheese, shredded
- 1/4 cup onion, diced
- 1/4 cup bell pepper, diced
- Salt, pepper, and garlic powder

Instructions:

1. Cook pasta and set aside.
2. Brown ground beef, then add onion and bell pepper, sautéing until softened.
3. Stir in sloppy joe sauce and simmer.
4. Mix in cooked pasta and top with cheddar cheese.
5. Bake at 375°F (190°C) for 15 minutes or until cheese is melted.

Ratatouille Mac

Ingredients:

- 1 lb elbow macaroni
- 1 zucchini, diced
- 1 eggplant, diced
- 1 bell pepper, diced
- 1 can diced tomatoes
- 1 cup mozzarella cheese, shredded
- 1 tbsp olive oil
- 1 tsp dried herbs (thyme, oregano, basil)
- Salt and pepper

Instructions:

1. Cook pasta and set aside.
2. Sauté zucchini, eggplant, bell pepper, and herbs in olive oil until softened.
3. Stir in diced tomatoes and season with salt and pepper.
4. Mix in pasta and top with mozzarella.
5. Bake at 375°F (190°C) for 15–20 minutes or until cheese is bubbly.

Pepperoni Pizza Mac

Ingredients:

- 1 lb elbow macaroni
- 1 cup marinara sauce
- 1 cup mozzarella cheese, shredded
- 1/2 cup pepperoni slices
- 1/4 cup Parmesan cheese, grated
- 1 tsp Italian seasoning

Instructions:

1. Cook pasta and set aside.
2. Stir marinara sauce into pasta, then mix in mozzarella, Parmesan, and Italian seasoning.
3. Top with pepperoni slices.
4. Bake at 375°F (190°C) for 15 minutes or until cheese is melted and bubbly.

Tex-Mex Mac Skillet

Ingredients:

- 1 lb elbow macaroni
- 1 lb ground beef or turkey
- 1 packet taco seasoning
- 1 can diced tomatoes with green chilies
- 1 cup cheddar cheese, shredded
- 1/4 cup sour cream
- Chopped green onions, for garnish
- 1/2 cup cilantro, chopped

Instructions:

1. Cook pasta and set aside.
2. Brown ground beef or turkey, then stir in taco seasoning and diced tomatoes.
3. Mix in cooked pasta, sour cream, and cheddar cheese.
4. Serve garnished with green onions and cilantro.

Mac and Cheese Stuffed Peppers

Ingredients:

- 4 bell peppers, tops removed and seeds scooped out
- 1 lb elbow macaroni
- 2 cups cheddar cheese, shredded
- 1/2 cup cream cheese
- 1/4 cup milk
- 1/2 cup breadcrumbs
- Salt and pepper

Instructions:

1. Cook pasta and set aside.
2. Mix cooked pasta with cream cheese, cheddar cheese, milk, salt, and pepper until creamy.
3. Stuff bell peppers with mac and cheese mixture.
4. Top with breadcrumbs and bake at 375°F (190°C) for 25–30 minutes or until peppers are tender.

Vegan Cashew Mac

Ingredients:

- 1 lb elbow macaroni
- 1 cup raw cashews, soaked for 4 hours
- 1/2 cup nutritional yeast
- 1/2 cup water or vegetable broth
- 1 tbsp lemon juice
- 1 tsp garlic powder
- Salt and pepper

Instructions:

1. Cook pasta and set aside.
2. Blend soaked cashews, nutritional yeast, water (or broth), lemon juice, garlic powder, salt, and pepper until smooth and creamy.
3. Mix in cooked pasta and serve warm.

Korean BBQ Mac

Ingredients:

- 1 lb elbow macaroni
- 1 lb beef short ribs or bulgogi beef, sliced
- 1/4 cup soy sauce
- 2 tbsp sesame oil
- 1 tbsp brown sugar
- 1 tbsp rice vinegar
- 2 cloves garlic, minced
- 1 tsp ginger, grated
- 1/2 cup shredded mozzarella cheese
- 1/4 cup green onions, chopped
- Sesame seeds for garnish

Instructions:

1. Cook pasta and set aside.
2. In a skillet, sauté beef with garlic, ginger, and sesame oil.
3. Stir in soy sauce, brown sugar, and rice vinegar, cooking until the beef is cooked through.
4. Mix in cooked pasta, then top with mozzarella cheese and green onions.
5. Garnish with sesame seeds and serve.

Gnocchi Mac and Cheese

Ingredients:

- 1 lb gnocchi
- 2 cups cheddar cheese, shredded
- 1/2 cup cream cheese
- 1/4 cup milk
- 1/2 cup Parmesan cheese, grated
- 1 tsp garlic powder
- Salt and pepper

Instructions:

1. Cook gnocchi according to package instructions and set aside.
2. In a saucepan, melt cream cheese and cheddar cheese with milk.
3. Stir in garlic powder, salt, and pepper.
4. Mix gnocchi with the cheese sauce, then top with Parmesan.
5. Serve immediately, garnished with additional cheese if desired.

Reuben Mac Casserole

Ingredients:

- 1 lb elbow macaroni
- 1/2 lb corned beef, chopped
- 1/2 cup sauerkraut, drained
- 1 cup Swiss cheese, shredded
- 1/2 cup Thousand Island dressing
- 1/2 cup breadcrumbs
- 1/4 cup butter, melted

Instructions:

1. Cook pasta and set aside.
2. Mix cooked pasta with corned beef, sauerkraut, Swiss cheese, and Thousand Island dressing.
3. Pour mixture into a casserole dish.
4. Top with breadcrumbs and melted butter.
5. Bake at 375°F (190°C) for 20–25 minutes or until golden and bubbly.

Mac and Cheese Egg Rolls

Ingredients:

- 1 lb elbow macaroni
- 2 cups cheddar cheese, shredded
- 1/4 cup cream cheese
- 1/4 cup milk
- 1/2 tsp garlic powder
- 1 package egg roll wrappers
- Oil for frying

Instructions:

1. Cook pasta and set aside.
2. In a saucepan, melt cream cheese and cheddar cheese with milk.
3. Mix in cooked pasta and garlic powder.
4. Spoon mac and cheese onto egg roll wrappers and roll them up tightly.
5. Fry in hot oil until golden brown. Serve with dipping sauce.

Fried Mac and Cheese Balls

Ingredients:

- 1 lb elbow macaroni
- 2 cups cheddar cheese, shredded
- 1/2 cup cream cheese
- 1/4 cup milk
- 1/4 cup Parmesan cheese, grated
- 1 egg, beaten
- 1/2 cup breadcrumbs
- Oil for frying

Instructions:

1. Cook pasta and set aside.
2. In a saucepan, melt cream cheese and cheddar cheese with milk.
3. Mix in cooked pasta and Parmesan, then let the mixture cool.
4. Roll the mac and cheese into small balls, dip in egg, and coat in breadcrumbs.
5. Fry in hot oil until golden brown, then drain on paper towels.

Mac and Cheese Waffles

Ingredients:

- 1 lb elbow macaroni
- 2 cups cheddar cheese, shredded
- 1/2 cup cream cheese
- 1/4 cup milk
- 1/4 cup breadcrumbs
- 1 egg, beaten
- 1 tsp garlic powder
- Salt and pepper

Instructions:

1. Cook pasta and set aside.
2. In a saucepan, melt cream cheese and cheddar cheese with milk.
3. Mix in cooked pasta, breadcrumbs, garlic powder, salt, and pepper.
4. Preheat a waffle iron and grease it lightly.
5. Spoon mac and cheese mixture into the waffle iron and cook until crispy.
6. Serve warm, optionally with a drizzle of hot sauce or BBQ sauce.

www.ingramcontent.com/pod-product-compliance
Lightning Source LLC
LaVergne TN
LVHW081326060526
838201LV00055B/2490